HAMISH McHAMISH

Susan McMullan is a fast-talking senior communications specialist and self-confessed grammar fiend.

Born and raised in Broughty Ferry, she is a graduate of the University of Dundee. She is fluent in French but less *au fait* with writing about herself in the third person.

Susan is married to a St Andrean and the couple live happily in the Auld Grey Toon with their not-so-famous but much-loved cat, Holly. *Hamish McHamish of St Andrews – Cool Cat About Town* is Susan's first book.

COOL CAT ABOUT TOWN

SUSAN McMULLAN

BLACK & WHITE PUBLISHING

First published 2012
by Black & White Publishing Ltd
29 Ocean Drive, Edinburgh EH6 6JL

5 7 9 10 8 6 4 14 15 16

ISBN: 978 1 84502 502 1

A CIP catalogue record for this book is available from the British Library.

Typeset by Creative Link, North Berwick
Printed and bound in Poland
www.hussarbooks.pl

For my wonderful husband Kevin, for his everlasting love and support.

A word from Hamish's Mum

Did you know that according to folklore no one can 'own' a cat? The saying recognises the fact that cats are independent free spirits. They may deign to keep you company, accept food and a warm place to sleep, but in the end it's up to them who they choose to view as their rightful owner, if anyone at all.

Hamish is the epitome of Kipling's 'cat that walks by himself', and over the years since I first brought him home as a tiny kitten, I've had to accept his choice of lifestyle! Once he had grown out of kittenhood, he decided my house and garden were far too small for his adventurous nature and he began his wandering ways. His absences from home became longer and longer, until he stopped visiting altogether.

I put up with the empty-nest syndrome for a few years but then succumbed to getting a resident dog and, understandably, since then Hamish has had a genuine excuse for never coming to visit – he scorns all dogs!

Once a year I have to initiate a search to find him so that I can take him to the vet for his annual health check. Thanks to the good folk of St Andrews, Hamish remains well-fed and healthy, although already approaching old age.

If he could speak, I don't think he would say, 'I belong to St Andrews', but rather, 'St Andrews belongs to me'!

Marianne Baird

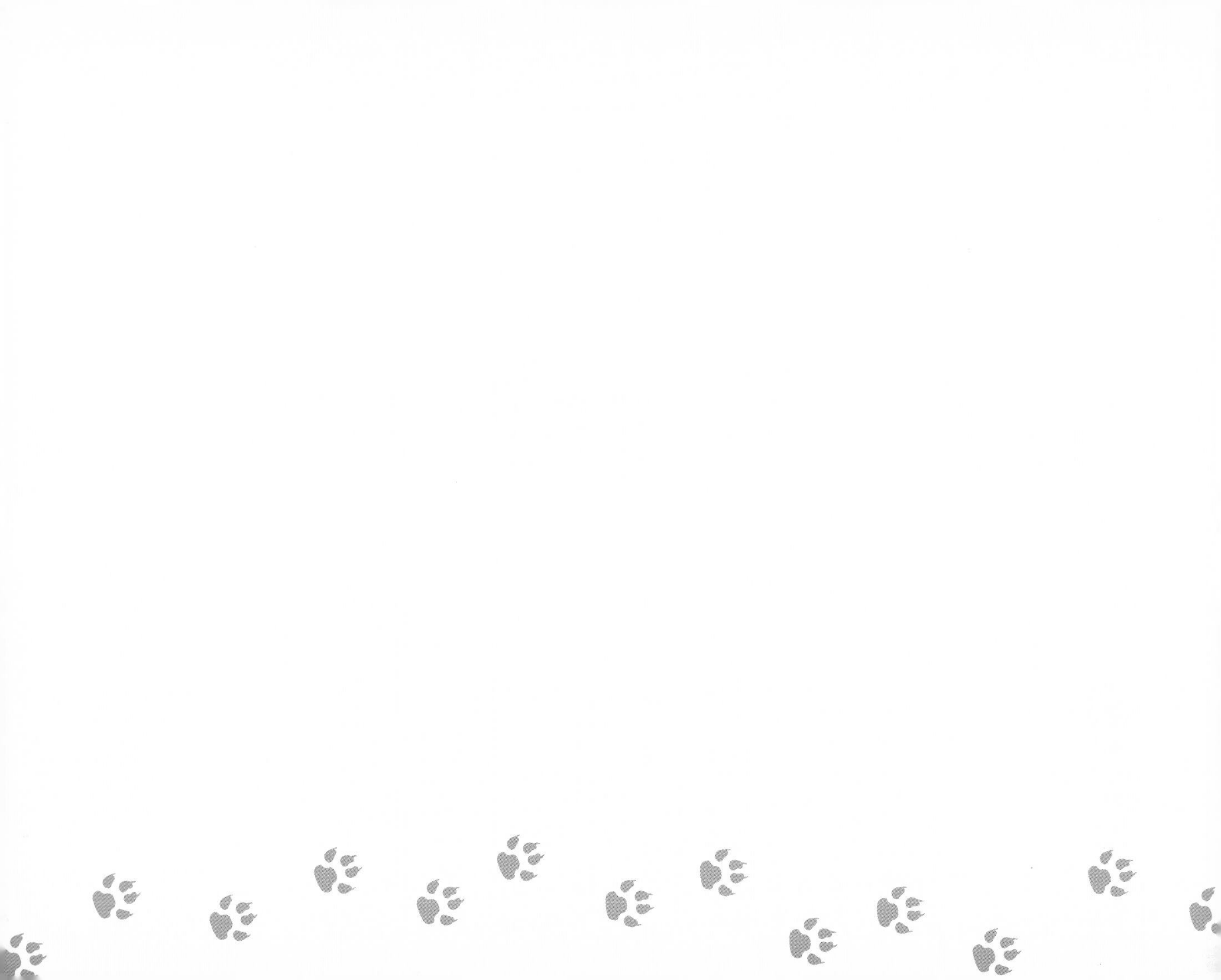

Introduction

With his fluffy white mane, shaggy ginger coat and big green eyes, it's obvious from the start that Hamish McHamish is no ordinary cat. Streetwise, savvy and fiercely intelligent, Hamish can hold his own in no uncertain terms. He's also hugely affectionate and generous with his time and friendship. With the loudest purr you're ever likely to hear, Hamish will melt your heart in an instant.

For the last thirteen years, Hamish has roamed the streets of St Andrews and lived his life his own way – as a cat about town. He has become something of a local legend and enjoys an almost celebrity-like status. Adored by St Andreans, students and tourists from all over the world, Hamish brings endless amounts of joy to the good folk of one of Scotland's most historic towns.

Everybody has their own story about Hamish; like the time he casually took on a fully-grown Labrador and won, just because he felt like it; or the moment he walked across the stage at Madras College in the middle of school assembly; the manner in which he simply wanders into any house he likes at any time and strolls around as if he owns the place and the way people just let him because he's Hamish McHamish, don't you know?

There's an unwritten rule in St Andrews: if Hamish appears at your door, always let him in. There's even a saying here that a shop can only be considered a true success once Hamish has called to say hello.

The sense of community that Hamish brings to St Andrews is undeniable. One glimpse at his Facebook page shows just how many people are brought together on a daily basis by the town's most famous feline resident. In a world of constant pressures and uncertainty, Hamish lifts people's spirits, makes people's days and brightens up the lives of even the most faithful of dog lovers. It's the simple pleasures that keep us all going, and there's something incredibly humbling about an animal that relies on the generosity of total strangers to get by. Hamish doesn't judge, doesn't differentiate between class or ethnicity, doesn't care if you're rich or poor, doesn't flinch if you're carrying a few extra pounds and isn't fussed whether you could give Einstein a run for his money or would prefer not to, thank you very much. Instead he lives unquestionably on the kindness and collective good of the human spirit.

I wrote this book because Hamish is a remarkable cat and deserves to be celebrated. The response I had while collecting Hamish's photographs was overwhelming. Everybody was tickled pink that he was to be honoured with his own book at last. Thank you to all those I worked with – you made this book possible, and for that I am ever grateful.

One of the other many highlights of writing this book was meeting Hamish's long-lost owner and hearing all her stories, including how Hamish actually came to be St Andrews' cat about town. Marianne is a lovely lady, whom I admire greatly. She cherishes Hamish very much but fully supports him in his wish to roam free. And so he does. Sometimes the handsome chap will stop long enough for her to say hello in passing, but then he's off again to see what other adventures the world has to offer.

Marianne trusts all of the people of St Andrews wholeheartedly to take good care of him, just as Hamish trusts them too. She chose Hamish because he was the boldest of the litter, and bold he certainly is.

The perfect tribute to the veritable King of St Andrews, this book should be shared and celebrated. So introduce Hamish to your friends, show him to your relatives or give him as a gift to your loved ones. Whatever you do, tell everyone you know about the glorious story of the lovable, huggable, wonderful . . . Hamish McHamish.

Here's to you, old friend!

Susan Elizabeth McMullan

Hello, my name is
Hamish McHamish.
I'm no ordinary cat.

You see, I'm a very famous cat and I live in the ancient town of St Andrews in Scotland.

This is my story.

It all started when I was just a kitten. Look at me when I was wee – as cute as cute can be!

Roar! I'm a big lion.

Sometimes even lions like
to sit in bidets.

Ever since I was little,
I knew I wanted to
be the most famous
cat of all.

So one day, I climbed into my mum's fireplace and all the way up the chimney onto the roof. Then I hopped into the tree in my garden . . .

... jumped over the wall ...

. . . and became Hamish McHamish – Cool Cat About Town. From that moment on, I've belonged to St Andrews and St Andrews has belonged to me.

There are lots of things to see and do in St Andrews. I spend most of my time roaming around, visiting shops and offices, saying hello to tourists and making new friends. I've got loads of them now, even on something called Facebook – whatever that is. Let me take you to some of my favourite places . . .

It's fun to visit the students at the University of St Andrews. They call me their study buddy. Did you know that the University of St Andrews is the oldest university in Scotland, and the third oldest in the English-speaking world, just after Oxford and Cambridge? Fancy!

The library is a warm place to go at night. With all those students working hard, it's the *purrfect* spot to *paws* for thought.

Here I am in St Salvator's Hall, keeping the students company. Sallies is where Prince William met Kate Middleton. If the Prince had liked cats better than Kates, things could have been so different!

This is me outside the University offices. Maybe one day I'll get an honorary degree.
St Katharine's West
16
Student Recruitment & Admissions
Exchanges & Study Abroad
Open Association
Corporate Communications

I really am very clever. I even know how to use zebra crossings.

At student parties I like to get dressed up and look the part.

Sometimes the students offer me a wee dram. They should know by now that I can't drink and meow!

I often pretend to be the tiger who came to tea. Mine's a milk – hold the sugar.
KEEP

Being a cat about town means I don't go home, so I like to visit my friends for dinner. Mum doesn't mind because she knows that the people of St Andrews are very kind to me and always give me delicious things to eat.

Like tasty smoked salmon.

And yummy tuna
and chicken.

I love going to this posh butcher to see what's on the menu. Mmm . . .

I'm quite partial to a steak bake or a sausage roll.

At the weekend I go for a Chinese takeaway . . .

...or for some Indian food . . .

. . . or for a burger or slice of pizza.
Cattro-formaggi, anyone?

This is Jannetta's – St Andrews' famous Italian ice cream parlour. Nothing better than a good slurp of ice cream on a hot day!

There are lots of coffee shops in St Andrews. I once had a girlfriend called Princess, but she stopped talking to me because I kept stealing her food. Maybe I should bring her here on a date. Looks like a romantic rendezvous.

I sometimes enjoy a spot of fine dining. This place really could use a cat flap. Just . . . can't . . . get . . . in . . .

In the mornings I do a bit of yoga.
It's important to be bendy.

Sunbathing in St Andrews is very relaxing. You have to be careful in the sun – especially if you have a big, beautiful, shaggy ginger coat like mine!

I like to get involved and give something back to the community. This is me helping the workmen re-lay the cobbles in Market Street, one of St Andrews' original medieval streets. Nice work, chaps!

Here I am doing a spot of campaigning to help Danielle run for physics president.

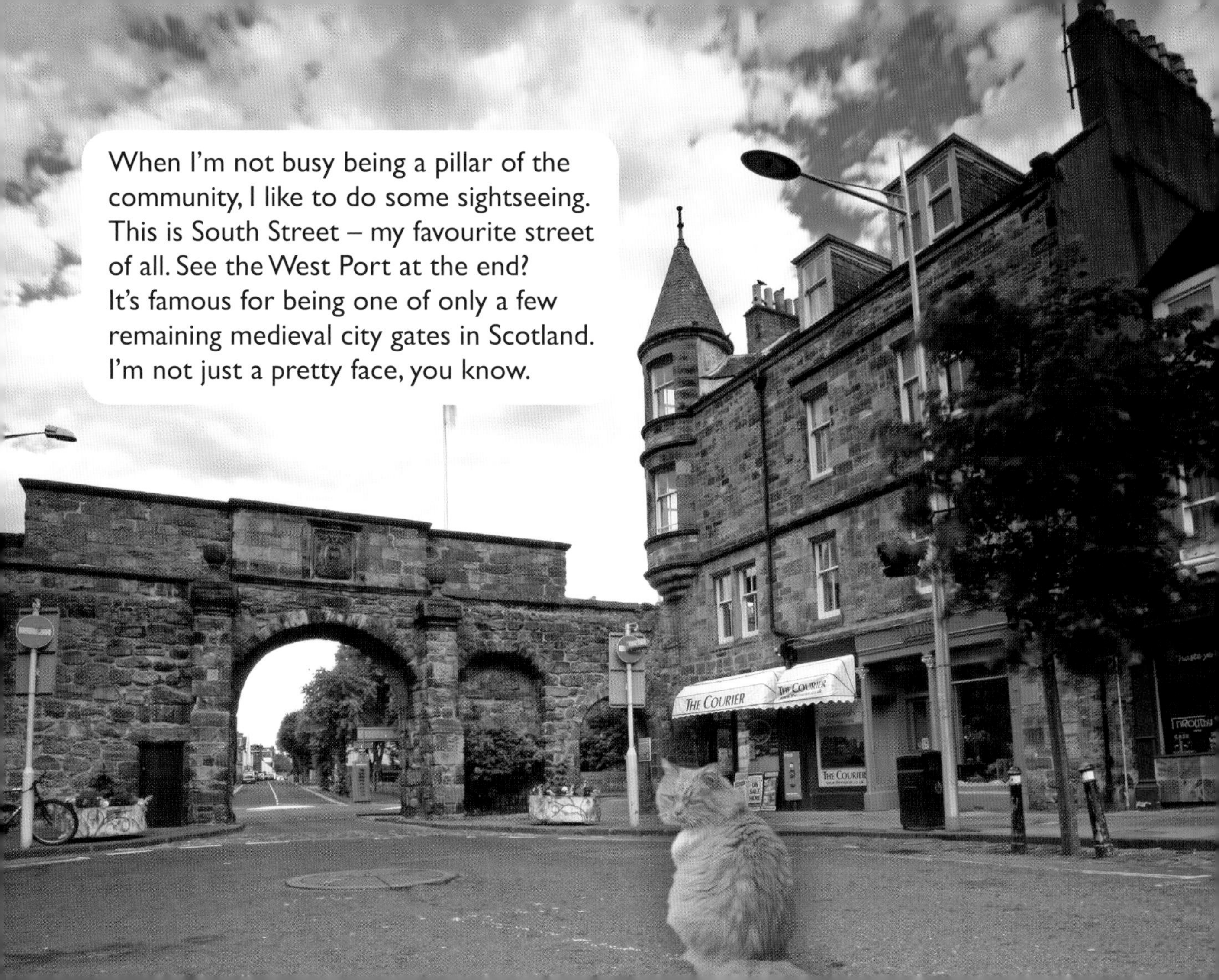
When I'm not busy being a pillar of the community, I like to do some sightseeing. This is South Street – my favourite street of all. See the West Port at the end? It's famous for being one of only a few remaining medieval city gates in Scotland. I'm not just a pretty face, you know.
THE COURIER
THE COURIER
THE COURIER

This is the Cathedral and
St Rule's Tower. You can climb
the stairs right to the top of the
Tower, but then you just have
to come all the way back down
again. Too much like hard work
for this old chap!

No matter how many times I visit St Andrews Castle, I can never quite muster up the courage to go down into the mines or bottle dungeon. They give me the heebie-jeebies!

Not far from the Castle is the famous West Sands beach that features in the opening scenes of the film *Chariots of Fire*. I do like to curl up in front of a good movie in the evening.

You can learn all about the history of St Andrews in the town's many museums. Maybe one day they'll open an exhibition on the exploits of Hamish McHamish?

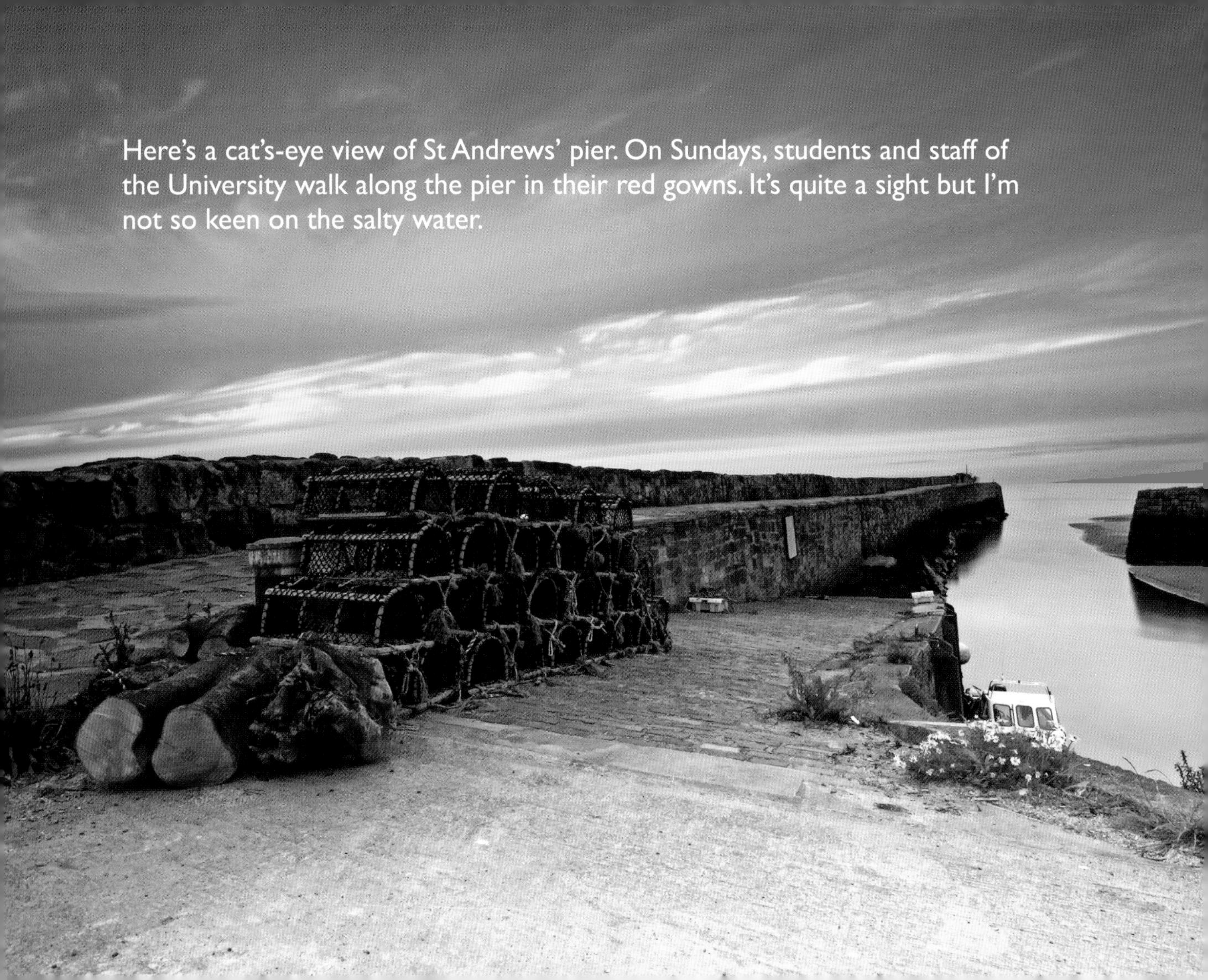

Here's a cat's-eye view of St Andrews' pier. On Sundays, students and staff of the University walk along the pier in their red gowns. It's quite a sight but I'm not so keen on the salty water.

I like to watch the weddings in St Salvator's Quad on a sunny day. On North Street, just as you go into the Quad, you'll see the letters PH in the cobbles. It's considered bad luck for students to walk across these letters, and it's said those who do will fail their final exams!

Living in the home of golf means I have to know my stuff. Golf has been played in St Andrews since the 1400s. This funny little bridge seems to be very popular.

This is the world-famous Old Course. It's a curious place where people hit a small white ball with a big stick – with unpredictable results.
For cats, it's a very dangerous place. For golfers' egos, it's not that safe either.

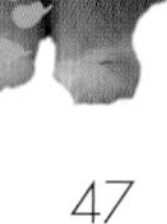

Down by the Old Course is Martyrs' Monument. It dates back to 1842 and symbolises the town's role in the Scottish Reformation. Maybe I should study *hiss-tory.*

Back in the centre of town you'll find the Whyte-Melville Memorial Fountain that commemorates the novelist George Whyte-Melville. Many people have said that this fountain should be replaced with a statue of me – it would be rude to disagree!

This is the Byre Theatre. It used to be a milking shed for cows, you know. I'm still waiting for the call asking me to be the lead role in one of their productions. *Puss in Boots* perhaps?

There are lots of lovely walks in St Andrews. This is me at the Kinness Burn, getting ready for a spot of fishing.

Pooches beware – this is my town!
It's a well-known fact that cats are much smarter than dogs. A dog will come to you when called. A cat will take a message and get back to you later.

When I'm not sightseeing, I like to call in at all the shops and offices in town. Everybody knows me and looks forward to my visits. Here I am in Waterstones bookshop, one of my favourite places.

I like the red zappy thing at the till.

These are my recommendations for the customers. You can't beat a good book!

Service with a purr!

Being this handsome and this clever is exhausting work!

Let sleeping cats lie.
It's important to snooze
whenever you can.

I like to sneak into people's houses to curl up all snug. The good folk of St Andrews don't mind me popping in for forty winks.

Flowerbeds are comfy too!

Of course, snoozing companions are always welcome.

Le Rendez - vous
Le chat s'assit sur le tapis. Impressive or what? People from all over the world visit St Andrews, so it's important that I lead a cosmopolitan lifestyle. Here I am brushing up on my French.

I make sure I'm well travelled . . .

I learn new traditions . . .

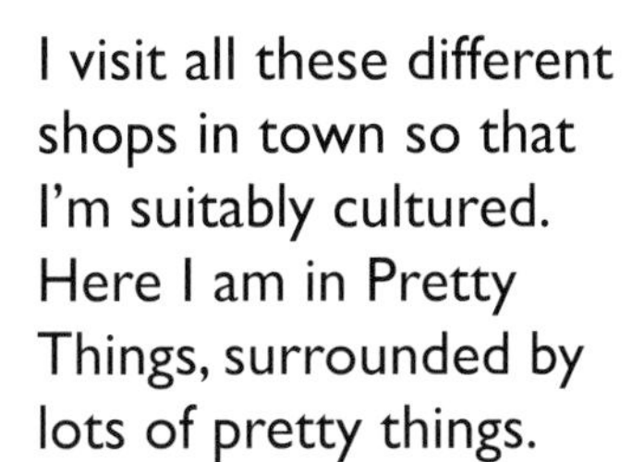

I visit all these different shops in town so that I'm suitably cultured. Here I am in Pretty Things, surrounded by lots of pretty things.

Only £5 in WH Smith – hope they don't mean me!

I have my own chair in lots of shops and offices in town. Here's my favourite hairdressers . . .

DYNAMIC HAIR
Welcome

This is my chair inside the hairdressers. The ladies brush my coat so that I always look my best.

I have my own big red comfy chair in Pagan Osborne, the house shop. The people there are very good to me, especially Pauline and Linda. They wash my blankets by hand because I don't like fabric softener. I'm a very particular cat.

I wait outside until the ladies see me and open the door to let me in. If there's nobody at the front door, I know to wait at the side door.

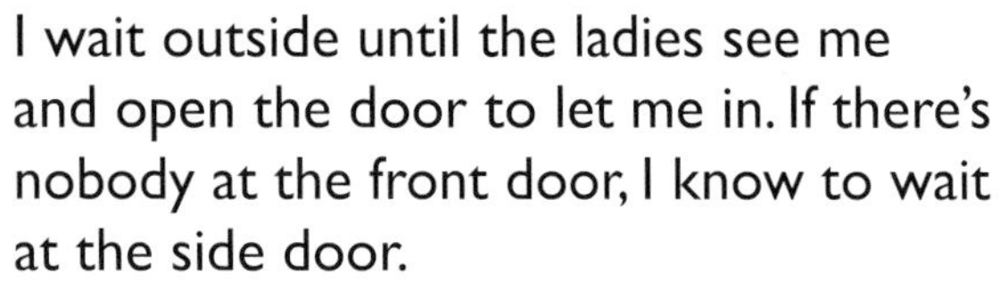

Here's me on my throne in another house shop called Bradburne & Co. What a big ball of fluff I am!

The ladies there let me help them with their work.

'Hello, Coolest Cat in Town speaking.'

At the Association for International Cancer Research offices, Dorothy gives me lots of jobs to do. My paws are a little too big for the computer keys though.

In Moshulu, the shoe shop, I get freshly prepared chicken, cooked to order. Yum!

This is one of my favourite chairs in the Sue Ryder charity shop.

And this is my other chair. It's a bit small, but I can just about squeeze on.

Here I am on my mat in the Sue Ryder shop. See, cats really do sit on mats.

Guest houses are good places to visit. The people in Nethan Guest House are always very welcoming, and they do a delicious breakfast.

In Brooksby Guest House the owners know exactly what I like for a midday snack – juicy prawns. Here I am next to the Aga in Brooksby in my post-prawn slumber.

The people in Aslar Guest House seem to like me quite a lot. It's not very often I smile for the camera.
Over the years I've perfected the impassive-as-a-sphinx look – just right for a Cool Cat About Town.

It's nice to be popular. Everywhere I go, tourists, students and St Andreans like to give me lots of hugs and have their photographs taken with me.

Big cuddles!

They do some funny poses.

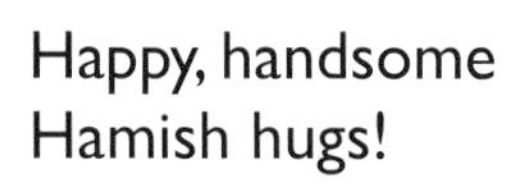

Happy, handsome Hamish hugs!

Hello, ladies!

What's new, pussycat?

A local reader sent in this charming photo and caption:

Badger the Standard Poodle, (a St Andrews resident) is introducing Ashley Kahrs, a visitor from Mountain View, California, to Hamish the town cat who was spotted in Queen's Gardens!

Our very own AristoCat, Hamish McHamish!

Chris Harris wrote:
"A warm summer's day round St Andrews seemed too much for this cat as I turned around to see him on the sofa upstairs in the office at Farmore Interiors. Its owner should consider purchasing the sofa since the cat seems particularly fond of it and no amount of stern talking proved to be enough for it to part from its fine taste in fabric."

Even the local magazine, *St Andrews in Focus*, likes to report sightings of me. The editor has been writing about me since 2006. She saw star quality in me from the beginning. Thanks, Flora!

St Andrews in focus · shopping · eating · events · town/gown · people and more

St Andrews – Home of Hamish

1\.

A Hamish Admirer writes:
" A 'dreich' day in St Andrews... Having escaped from the rain, along with many humans – the Sue Ryder shop was rather full – Hamish found that he'd exchanged one trying circumstance for another. Whilst trying to have a quick brush-up and rearrange his damp fur he found some young admirers attentive for rather too long, hence the somewhat discountenanced demeanour!"

2\. Lorraine, another admirer, caught Hamish having a brief lie-down in South Street.

I saw Hamish wandering about Madras College recently and wondered if he was looking for an education. Alas, I'd left my camera at home. However.....

Ann Wharmby sent in this charming study. She says that she found Hamish reposing in the Sue Ryder charity shop in Logie's Lane.

Please send in your photos of Hamish, and tell us where you've seen him, and what you know about him.

In fact, some people call me the King of St Andrews!

Throughout all of my travels though, what I like most of all is to watch over the Auld Grey Toon. St Andrews is very important to me. It's my home and all its people are my friends.

The next time you visit St Andrews, be sure to take a look around all of my favourite places. I hope you love this town as much as I do.

Hamish's Credits and Acknowledgements

All the fabulous scenic photography in my book is courtesy of the very lovely Charlotte of Charlotte Brett Photography: www.charlottebrettphotography.co.uk.

A thousand thank yous to my good friend Emma Haxton for creating my Facebook page and introducing me to lots of wonderful people.

Equally big purrs for the splendid Flora Selwyn, founder and editor of the award-winning magazine *St Andrews in Focus*. She was single-handedly responsible for my rise to fame and has always kept the good people of St Andrews up-to-date on my adventures: www.standrewsinfocus.com.

Exclusive Hamish hugs to all of my Facebook friends, old and new, who very kindly supplied their photographs for my book. Here are your names on my wall of fame! It's a long list – you might need to put the kettle on.

Adam Moran
AICR St Andrews – Dorothy Titterton, Suzanne Shaw
Alasdair Johnston
Alex Kekewich
Alexandra Jean Harper
Alexander Mason
Alison Brown
Andrew Jaberoo
Angela Jackson
Anna Kucharska
Anna Moles
Arsa Syed
Ashley Cole
Aslar Guest House – Sarah Southall, Katherine Palfrey
Barbara McNeilly
Becky Ballantyne
Ben Brown
Bianca Maya Brown
Bradburne & Co – Alison Brown
Britt McCray
Brooksby Guest House – Caryn Beaton
Caitlin Carty
Catherine Suzanne Barbour
Chendi Hu
Chess Jaconelli
Christopher Impiglia
Courtney Scovel
Dan Labriola
Dainius Macikenas
Danielle Harper

David Bantel
Deirdre Mitchell
Diana Drumm
Dynamic Hair – Paula Baker
Eleanor Campbell
Elizabeth Wiebe
Emma Lister
Fiona Don
Francesca Vaghi
Gillian Patterson
Jackie Buist
Jane Rice
Jennifer F. Grant
Jens Munthe
Ka Wing Chan
Kat Scott
Kevin McMullan
Kevin O'Neill
Kirsteen Runcie
Kirstie Read
Klára Žvejklárka
Kristy Ettles
Laura Sneddon
Lauren Allison
Le Rendezvous
Lewis Fairfax
Lisa Crichton
Louise Lane
Lyndsay Mitchell
M Alexandra Bomphray
Madeleine Otto
Maxwell Greenberg
Minick of St Andrews – Stuart Minick
Misha Iasinskyi
Morgan Price
Moshulu
Nethan Guest House – Rebecca Taylor Linzi Taylor
Nicole Judd
Noah Ohringer
Noronha Concepta
Owen Williams
Pagan Osborne – Linda Black, Pauline Mackenzie-Dodds, Neil Fyall, Rebecca Richmond
Pamela Davidson
Paraskevi Niki Lampri
Phillip Goose
Pollyanna Delany
Pretty Things – Irene J M Harley
Psalm Moatari
Robert Evans
Robert Llyod
Rory Alexander Greig
Siannie Moodie
Siobhan King
Siti Sabariah
Sophia Nestius-Brown
Stephanie Barrie
Susannah Raymond-Barker
Tanya Bykova
Urte Macikenaite
Wendy Gong
William Staff

If you liked my book, come and join me on Facebook for all my latest updates. See you soon!